My Brother's Motorcycle

Written by
Claudette C. Mitchell, Gracie R. Porter and Patricia Tefft Cousin
Illustrated by
James R. Threalkill and Michael J. McBride

ARBORLAKE
PUBLISHING

My brother's motorcycle
has big handlebars.

My brother's motorcycle
has a clear windshield.

My brother's motorcycle has a long seat.

My brother's motorcycle has a loud motor.

My brother's motorcycle has a shiny tailpipe.

My brother's motorcycle
has two black wheels.

And mine does too.